# Directions In Art

# Sculp

D0245694

Jillian Powell

Heinemann
LIBRARY

**www.heinemann.co.uk/library**
Visit our website to find out more information about Heinemann Library books.

To order:
☎ Phone 44 (0) 1865 888066
📠 Send a fax to 44 (0) 1865 314091
💻 Visit the Heinemann Bookshop at www.heinemann.co.uk/library to browse our catalogue and order online.

First published in Great Britain by Heinemann Library, Halley Court, Jordan Hill, Oxford OX2 8EJ, part of Harcourt Education.
Heinemann is a registered trademark of Harcourt Education Ltd.

© Harcourt Education Ltd 2003
First published in paperback in 2004
The moral right of the proprietor has been asserted.

Editorial: Lucy Thunder and Helen Cannons
Design: Jo Hinton-Malivoire and AMR
Picture Research: Hannah Taylor and Elaine Willis
Production: Edward Moore

Originated by Ambassador Litho Ltd
Printed and bound in China by South China Printing Company

ISBN 0 431 17642 6 (hardback)
07 06 05 04 03
10 9 8 7 6 5 4 3 2 1

ISBN 0 431 17652 3 (paperback)
08 07 06 05 04
10 9 8 7 6 5 4 3 2 1

**British Library Cataloguing in Publication Data**
Powell, Jillian
Sculpture. – (Directions in art)
730.9
A full catalogue record for this book is available from the British Library.

**Acknowledgements**
The Publishers would like to thank the following for permission to reproduce photographs: AKG Photo / Jurgen Raible © Louise Bourgeois / VAGA, New York / DACS, London 2003 p**9**; Annebicque Bernard / Corbis Sygma p**32**; Bettmann / Corbis / Tom Salver p**7**; Louise Bourgeois Courtesy of Cheim & Read © Louise Bourgeois / VAGA, New York / DACS, London 2003 p**10**; Bridgeman Art Library / Mattiolo Collection, Milan, Italy p**6**; Camera press / Richard Open p**43**; Corbis / Layne Kennedy p**41**; Sokari Douglas Camp p**15**; Sokari Douglas Camp / British Museum p**13**; Sokari Douglas Camp / Sharon Hollingsworth p**14**; Richard Glover 2002 p**44**; Andy Goldsworthy pp**17**, **18**, **19**; Antony Gormley / Sally Ann Norman Courtesy of Gateshead Council p**21**; Antony Gormley / Courtesy Jay Jopling, London p**23**; Damien Hirst p**27**; Courtesy Jay Jopling / White Cube p**25**; Anish Kapoor Courtesy of Lisson Gallery p**29**; David Mach Courtesy of Galerie Jérôme de Noirmont, Paris pp**31**, **33**; Musee Picasso, Paris / Beatrice Hatala © Succession Picasso / DACS 2003 p**4**; Anthony Oliver, Courtesy Jay Jopling / White Cube p**26**; Cornelia Parker / Tate Picture Library p**35**; Cornelia Parker / Victoria and Albert Museum p**37**; Rex Features / The Stewart Bonney Agency p**22**; Estate of Robert Smithson, Courtesy James Cohan Gallery, New York. Collection: DIA Center for the Arts, New York. Photo by Gianfranco Gorgoni © Estate of Robert Smithson / VAGA, New York / DACS, London 2003 p**39**; Madeline Wiener pp**47**, **48**.

Cover photograph of *House* by Rachel Whiteread (1993) reproduced with permission of Corbis/ Richard Glover.

The Publishers would like to thank Richard Stemp, Gallery Educator at the Tate in London, for his assistance in the preparation of this book.

Every effort has been made to contact copyright holders of any material reproduced in this book. Any omissions will be rectified in subsequent printings if notice is given to the Publishers.

**Disclaimer**
All the internet addresses (URLs) given in this book were valid at the time of going to press. However, due to the dynamic nature of the Internet, some addresses may have changed, or sites may have changed or ceased to exist since publication. While the author and Publisher regret any inconvenience this may cause readers, no responsibility for any such changes can be accepted by either the author or the Publishers.

# CONTENTS

Any words appearing in the text in bold, **like this**, are explained in
the Glossary.

# DIRECTIONS IN SCULPTURE

Today we can see sculpture all around us, not just in museums and galleries, but in the street, by motorways, in shopping centres and even as part of the landscape. For hundreds of years, sculpture was traditionally seen in churches, public buildings and parks, often in the form of monuments or memorials. **Relief sculptures** decorated the front of buildings and statues were displayed in alcoves in the walls of galleries and private houses. Sculptors used three main techniques – **carving** in stone, ivory or wood, **modelling** in clay, wax and plaster, and **casting** in bronze and lead. Their main subject was the human body, often represented in **commemorative** or religious works.

## Changing forms and techniques

At the beginning of the 20th century, young artists began to experiment with new ideas, **forms** and techniques. Instead of studying **classical sculpture**, they looked to new influences like folk and tribal art. Pablo Picasso (1881–1973) and Paul Gauguin (1848–1903) were inspired by the strong, simple forms of tribal art. They looked at the forms of tribal objects, like masks, carved into strong angular shapes using simple hand tools. These influences encouraged Picasso and Gauguin to move away from the human figure towards more **abstract** forms. They also began to experiment with the materials they used, inspired by the way tribal artists combined different materials, some of which were perishable, such as feathers, leaves, tree bark and paper.

*Picasso used a bicycle seat and handlebars to create this bronze cast called* Bull's Head *(1943).*

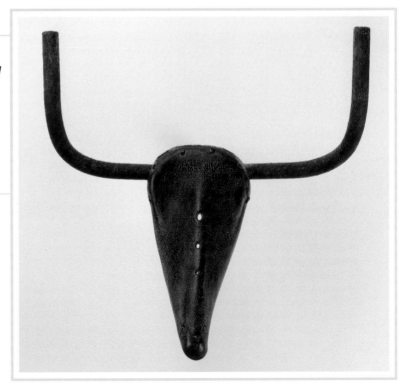

Even the concept of what makes a sculpture was challenged when, in 1917, the artist Marcel Duchamp (1887–1968) exhibited a urinal from a gents' toilet under the title *Fountain*.

> *I am interested in ideas, not merely in visual products.*
> MARCEL DUCHAMP

By exhibiting a ready-made object as a sculpture, Duchamp introduced the idea that the artist's concept was more important than technical or manual skills: a bicycle wheel stuck on a kitchen stool could be art. Picasso and others began to explore ways of assembling sculptures using 'found objects' such as old saucepans, wheels and other pieces of junk (see picture on page 4). A new method of creating sculpture – **construction** or **assemblage** – extended the range of forms available to sculptors.

## Picasso's Guitar 1914

Pablo Picasso was an endlessly inventive artist. With his *Guitar*, he introduced a new concept of sculpture. Until then, sculpture meant solid forms and continuous surfaces. Picasso cut and folded sheets of metal then welded them together to create an open, hollow form, suggesting the sound hole of a stringed instrument. This began a trend of 'open form' sculptures that spread from Russian Constructivism to the works of Anthony Caro (b. 1924) in Britain.

## New materials

As different movements swept through the art world – **Cubism**, **Futurism**, **Constructivism**, **Surrealism** – sculptors responded with new forms and materials. The Futurist Umberto Boccioni (1882–1916) tried representing movement with multi-faceted forms, and suggested using devices such as electric motors and lights to bring sculpture alive.

The Russian Constructivist Naum Gabo (1890–1977) made sculptures using modern materials like transparent plastics, glass and industrial sheets of steel. New engineering techniques such as welding improved structural strength, allowing sculptors to experiment with open, abstract forms that appeared light and weightless. Space became an important element in design as sculptors began to create works that enclosed space as well as being surrounded by it.

*In this sculpture,* Muscular Dynamism *or* Unique Forms of Continuity in Space *(1913), Umberto Boccioni tried to capture a figure in motion by using broken, flame-like forms. Each part of the figure is multi-faceted – it has many faces that catch the light in different ways, seeming to flicker like a moving picture as you move around the sculpture. The dynamic figure stands astride two bases, further adding to the sense of forward movement.*

## New trends

In the 1950s, the centre of the art world moved from Paris to New York. Many European artists had emigrated there after World War II and the growing wealth of the United States meant there were more **patrons** looking for art to decorate their homes and offices. New trends included **Pop Art**, **Minimalism** and **Conceptual Art**. In Pop Art, sculptors and painters worked with familiar everyday materials like food cans and plastics. Minimalist artists worked with pure geometric forms. Conceptual artists pursued Duchamp's idea that the concept was all-important: anything could be exhibited as art if the artist saw it that way.

Artists began to change the way viewers looked at their work. **Installation Art** grew out of the **Performance Art** and **Happenings** of the 1960s. For **installations**, artists used their gallery or exhibition space to involve the public in their work. For example, Carl André (b. 1935) used piles of bricks or industrial steel to divide up the gallery space, so that the viewer could walk through, around and over his sculpture rather than just standing in front of it.

Other artists, like Robert Smithson (see pages 38–41) and Andy Goldsworthy (see pages 16–19) rejected traditional viewing places like galleries and museums and took their sculpture outside to create **Land Art**. Smithson's larger projects involved many workers and even earth-moving machines. They were designed to change with time and the weather. 'Christo' (real name Christo Javacheff, b. 1935) developed 'Packaging Art' using modern sheet materials to wrap large objects such as trees, cars, buildings and even whole islands or areas of land. Photography and film are the only ways of making these sculptures last, except in the memories of viewers.

## Using new materials and technology

In the last twenty years, sculptors have experimented with a wide range of synthetic and industrial fibres and metals, including steel, cement, perspex and resin, and even newspaper and domestic rubbish. Claes Oldenburg (b. 1929) made a sculpture called *Wedding Souvenir* (1996), from slices of wedding cake moulded from Plaster of Paris. Helen Chadwick (1953–96) made a sculpture out of bubbling chocolate: a fountain filled the gallery with the smell of cocoa. Some artists work on industrial-scaled projects, using digital technology and high-tech engineering. Others re-interpret traditional skills using new materials, such as casting in resin rather than bronze.

At the beginning of the 21st century, computer technology continues to influence the design, engineering and construction of sculpture. Sculptors may work with experts in other fields such as computer modellers, engineers and industrial manufacturers to create their works. Sculptures are no longer confined to alcoves and plinths. They occupy space aggressively, encouraging us to experience them interactively.

The sculptors featured in this book represent the wide range of working methods and materials used today. Some draw on traditional ideas and techniques; others are breaking new ground with their subject matter and methods of construction. Some works are controversial because of their subject matter, like Damien Hirst's *The Impossibility of Death in the Mind of Someone Living*, which features a dead Tiger Shark (see pages 26–27), others for their form and appearance, like Antony Gormley's vast jet-winged *Angel of the North* (see pages 21–23). They all invite us to look at sculpture with new eyes.

'Christo' and Jeanne-Claude wrapped islands off the coast of Florida in pink plastic from 1980 to 1983 to create Surrounded Islands.

# LOUISE BOURGEOIS

Louise Bourgeois is a French-American sculptor who was born in Paris in 1911. As a child she sometimes helped out in the workshop that her parents ran, restoring antique tapestries. Her childhood was disrupted by the death of her mother when Louise was just 8 years old. Bourgeois decided to study Maths at the Sorbonne university in Paris, before switching to Art. She studied under Marcel Duchamp (see page 5) and became interested in the ideas of **Cubism** and **Surrealism**.

In 1938, Bourgeois moved to the Unites States and became an American citizen. She began doing paintings and engravings, but turned to sculpture in the late 1940s. She did not become famous until she was 71 years old, when she held a **retrospective** exhibition at the Museum of Modern Art in New York.

## Ideas and aims

Bourgeois began making sculptures that carried symbolic references to her own life, and in particular the emotions she felt during childhood. Her early sculptures are groups of **abstract** and **organic** shapes, often carved from wood. In 1949, she exhibited a group of black forms carved from wood, called *Personnages*. They represented the family and people she had left behind in France.

> *My childhood has never lost its magic, it has never lost its mystery, and it has never lost its drama. Everything I create comes from something personal; some memory or emotional experience.*
> LOUISE BOURGEOIS

## Techniques and approach

From the 1960s, Bourgeois began exploring materials such as bronze, stone, plaster and latex rubber. Her techniques include **carving**, **casting**, welding and **assemblage**. In her later works she turned to room-sized **installations** and huge works constructed in fabrics. These installations can include tall towers that viewers can climb, metal sculptures that they can walk under and through, and cages they can walk around and peer into. This makes Bourgeois' works interactive, so viewers participate and become part of them.

## Maman

In 1999, Bourgeois was **commissioned** to create a large scale installation for the long Turbine Hall in the Tate Modern in London. This was the setting for her famous spider sculpture, the giant *Maman*. Although *Maman* represents a mother figure (the title means mummy in French), the spider is a brown recluse spider, which is poisonous.

## Symbolism of spiders

With the creation of *Maman*, Bourgeois returned to ideas and images that had strong symbolic meaning for her. Her family connections with weaving and tapestries inspired her fascination with nature's weaver, the spider. For Bourgeois, spiders are a symbol of women's powers and skills. They weave their intricate webs, just as women are skilled knitters and weavers. She also sees them as protective mother figures, laying and guarding their eggs. However, they have a more sinister side – the spider lures its prey to its web and traps it.

*(My mother) was also intelligent, patient, clear and useful, reasonable, subtle and indispensable as a spider.* LOUISE BOURGEOIS

*This sketch of a spider by Bourgeois (2002) is one of many that she has drawn.*

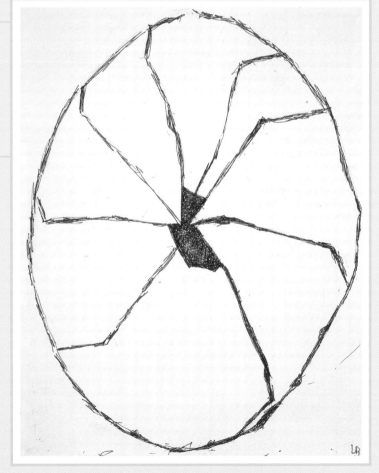

# A giant structure

Bourgeois began her work for *Maman* by making a series of drawings, annotated with notes. She used these notes and drawings to explore the **form** and structure of the sculpture. *Maman* stands 10 metres high and is made from welded steel and marble. The body is shaped like a dome and made from cones of metal ore twisted round a basket of steel. It protects a mesh sack containing white marble eggs. Each of the eight legs is made from tubular steel welded to the body, coloured with a bronze stain or 'patina'. The legs are formed into arches that rest on tiny points bolted into the floor. They create a space which viewers can walk underneath: making sculpture into architecture. Bourgeois has constructed the whole so that you can see the separate parts, and the seams where steel has been welded together.

The sculpture stood near three tall towers made from concrete, steel and brick. The towers were called *I do, I undo* and *I redo*. Each tower supported a platform surrounded by mirrors. Viewers could climb spiral staircases on the towers and sit in these mirrored spaces, encountering strangers or friends on their way down and reflecting while looking through the mirrors.

## More mirrors

Mirrors are also used in Bourgeois' series of works called *Cells* (1990–93). These are cage-like spaces that contain objects and light effects capturing different moods and emotions. They are constructed from steel, painted aluminium, glass, mirrors, electric lights and water. The mirrors encourage viewers to look at themselves, at other aspects of the work or its content, and at other onlookers sharing the space. The reflections change as viewers come and go, making Bourgeois' work alive and interactive.

## Influences

In the early 1930s, Bourgeois travelled to Russia as a student and saw the works of the Russian **Constructivist** sculptors, Vladimir Tatlin (1885–1953), Naum Gabo and Antoine Pevsner (1886–1962). They were challenging old ideas of sculpture by using modern materials like plastics, glass and sheets of metal to create open, transparent structures that had separate, moveable parts.

Bourgeois also became interested in the works of European **Surrealist** artists who had emigrated to America after the World War II. Artists like Salvador Dali (1904–89) used dreams as a source of ideas for works that were often visually surprising and unsettling – like a telephone with a lobster as a handset. They were using sculptures to suggest ideas rather than to represent something.

# Sokari DOUGLAS CAMP

Sokari Douglas Camp is a Kalabari sculptor who lives and works in London. She was born in 1958 in Bugama, Nigeria and grew up in the Niger Delta. She trained at Dartington College in England before going to the California College of Art and Craft in the United States. In 1983, Douglas Camp went on to the Central School of Art and Design in London, and three years later completed a Master of Arts degree in Sculpture at the Royal College of Art. She has exhibited her works in Britain, America, New Zealand and Japan.

## Combining traditional and modern

Douglas Camp is known for her **figurative** metal sculptures that combine traditional tribal images with modern materials and techniques. Douglas Camp's work reflects the rich culture of the Kalabari people who live on the islands of the Niger Delta, where they have fished and traded for centuries. Her sculptures acknowledge the African concept that art objects should have a purpose, whether it is domestic, religious or educational. Much of her work is inspired by the traditional dance and music performances of the Masquerade. The Masquerades are traditional Kalabari performances of dance and music that celebrate the passing of the seasons in the agricultural year, and also mark the passing from boyhood to manhood for young men of the tribe. Her Masquerade figures represent the culture and traditions of the Kalabari people.

African art has been an important influence on modern art. This can be seen through the works of 20th century artists including Henri Matisse (1869–1954) André Derain (1880–1954) Pablo Picasso and Georges Braque (1882–1963).

## Big Masquerade with Boat and Household on his Head

In the 1980s, Douglas Camp began to make sculptures inspired by the Masquerade tradition of the Kalabari. In Kalabari culture, it is only the men who are allowed to make the masks and costumes and perform in the Masquerades. For the Kalabari, as for other west African coastal peoples, the local swamps and creeks are the home of spiritual beings. During the Masquerade, the Kalabari men dress up in costumes and masks that represent the water spirits. They call on the spirits to possess them as they perform the Masquerade to traditional dance and drum music.

One of Douglas Camp's most elaborate pieces inspired by the Masquerades is *Big Masquerade with Boat and Household on his Head*, which was made in 1995. The figure represents one of the most important and fierce spirits called up during the Masquerades. He is made from steel, wood, cloth, paint and feather dusters. He is shown carrying two sharp swords, and wearing an apron stained with blood. He stands with his arms outstretched, holding a sword in each hand, and leaning forward in a menacing way.

The wooden boat and household on his head are symbols of his wealth. In Kalabari society, a man's wealth is measured by how many people are housed under his roof. Every powerful household also has a war canoe, and paddlers who can steer it around the Niger Delta. The boat is a simpler version of an original Kalabari carving, and Douglas Camp has inscribed it with words written to her niece. It is painted with 'Robin blue', a pigment bought at Nigerian markets to bleach laundry.

## Tools and techniques

Douglas Camp's figures are lifesize and constructed from steel, welded together in jointed sections. This copies the way African ancestral figures and headpieces are made in jointed parts. The joints mean that different sections can move, giving the sculpture a lively quality that reflects the nature of the Masquerades. Douglas Camp has also experimented with electric motors that set the sculpture in motion. Some spin round, as if dancing in a trance state, others beat drums. This creates movement and dynamism.

*Douglas Camp works with modern power tools to weld metal parts of her figures.*

## Kinetic Art

**Kinetic Art** uses technology, movement and light to create changing, dynamic forms. The concept was first developed by the Russian **Constructivists** Naum Gabo and Antoine Pevsner in the 1920s. They believed sculpture did not need a definite, solid appearance. Artwork could take form through Kinetic Art: for example, by taking a piece of string which was weighted at one end, and making it spin at the other end, a sculpture could be created by the spinning shape.

In the 1950s and 60s, artists working in Europe and the USA began to develop Kinetic Art. Some, like Alexander Calder (1898–1976), used natural forces of air, wind and gravity to create movement in mobile sculptures; others, like Pol Bury (b. 1922), experimented with electric motors to rotate and move sculptures.

## Performance rather than display

Douglas Camp's works are partly a reaction against the western practice of displaying African masks and other pieces in galleries and museums, away from their true context as part of **Performance Art**. Her figures are often shown in exhibitions alongside authentic masks and headpieces, with videos of the Masquerade performance of dance and music.

> *Performance, not sculpture, is the highest form of art in west Africa. That's a foreign concept in the West.* SOKARI DOUGLAS CAMP

Douglas Camp's Masquerade figures wear colourful replicas of the costumes and masks made by the Kalabari. She decorates them with many different materials including wood, feathers, mirrors, ceremonial cloth, tinsel and Christmas tree baubles. She also uses the wicker baskets woven by the Kalabari for storage vessels, fish traps and drying racks. Many pieces are directly inspired by originals in museum collections. *Naked Fish* (1998), copies an old Masquerade head piece in the British Museum in London. It is constructed from a wicker basket which was made to carry fish or periwinkles, with a fish carved from wood tied on top.

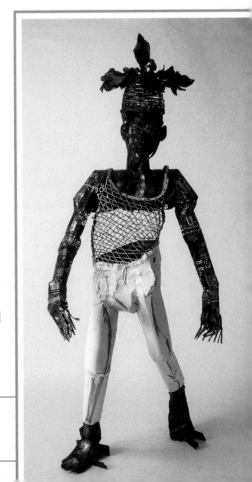

## Influences

The materials and techniques Douglas Camp uses show the influence of western artists such as the American Richard Serra (b. 1939) and the British sculptor Sir Anthony Caro (b. 1924). Caro and Serra began using industrial materials and techniques to create metal sculptures in the 1960s. Caro trained as an engineer before becoming a sculptor. He created metal sculptures by welding together materials like steel plates, propeller blades and aluminium tubing. Serra had worked in a steel mill and in the 1960s he began using steel and lead to create huge **Minimalist** sculptures which were held in place only by their weight and gravity.

Naked Fish *(1998) wears a string vest and carries a fish basket on his head.*

# ANDY GOLDSWORTHY

Andy Goldsworthy is famous for creating '**site specific**' works. He was born in Cheshire, England in 1956 and grew up in Yorkshire. He studied Art at Bradford College of Art (1974–75) and Preston Polytechnic (1975–78). After college, he lived in Yorkshire, Lancashire and Cumbria, moving over the border into Scotland in the mid 1980s.

## Site specific works

Since the 1970s, most of Goldsworthy's works have been created in the open air, in remote places ranging from the Yorkshire Dales and the Lake District, to the North Pole and the Australian Outback. These are 'site specific' works, made from natural materials from the remote locations he visits, so in the Arctic he made arches from snow and ice and in the north of England he worked with local stone and chalk. Many of his materials are perishable, such as twigs, leaves, snow and ice, reeds and thorns. Goldsworthy enjoys creating works with his own hands, although for some of his larger projects he uses assistants and even large plant machinery.

## Ideas and forms

Often, Goldsworthy's works are based on natural, **organic** shapes – spirals, circles, and undulating, or curving, lines. Some of his sculptures encircle a natural object such as a tree trunk or boulder; others hang from or lead up to the natural **form**. He plays with colour and light and shadow, and sees colour as a kind of energy, especially as the colours in nature are always changing.

> *When I covered a rock with leaves, it was to touch the autumns that the rock had witnessed. And when I covered the rock with red or yellow, it's not like painting a surface onto the rock; it's to touch the energy within that rock.* ANDY GOLDSWORTHY

Goldsworthy's works can be seen as '**interventions**' in the natural landscape: he draws the shape of a river on a flat stone placed in water, or he arranges yellow and red leaves in the hollow of a rock, or attaches leaves and foliage to a tree trunk. He is interested in the 'movement, light, growth and decay' of nature, and emphasizes the changing seasons, weather and landscape in his works. As many of the natural materials he uses will melt, blow away or decay, most of his works only last a short time. These are called 'ephemeral works.'

> *You must have something new in a landscape as well as something old, something that's dying and something that's being born.* ANDY GOLDSWORTHY

## Ephemeral works

Goldsworthy's ephemeral works include a tower of stones built on a beach at low tide, where the action of the waves would topple the stones as the tide came in, and icicles moulded into a spiral around the trunk of a tree. *Rain Shadows* was a series of works created in countries including France, the United States, Denmark and Australia. To make them, the artist lay down on the pavement during a downpour of rain, leaving a dry shape outlining his body. At the Barbican in London, Goldsworthy got workmen to slap slabs of clay onto a huge wall, to make a *London Wall* which would crack and crumble like a desert as it dried out.

For his 'ephemeral performance sculptures', Goldsworthy throws materials such as sand, water or earth into the air: these works last only a few moments so they have to be recorded in photographs. Goldsworthy documents and photographs all his works in books which act as lasting records of his work.

In his more recent works, Goldsworthy has begun to use more permanent materials. For his *Sheepfolds* (1996–2000) project in Cumbria, he worked with local dry-stone wallers, building and repairing about a hundred sheepfolds – the looping, dry-stone walls used in open country to round up sheep. He also planted trees, and placed arches, cairns (piles of stones that act as landmarks) and boulders in and around the old walls.

*Here a line of dry stone walling snakes around trees in Goldsworthy's* Storm King *project (1997–1998).*

## Influences

In the 20th century, sculptors began working directly with the environment, moving sculpture out of galleries and museums into the landscape. In site specific works, the setting is all-important to the artist, influencing the **form** and meaning of the work. Henry Moore (1898–1986) was one of the first sculptors to involve the natural setting with the form of his works. He placed sheep sculptures in fields where real sheep wandered between them. Working with the natural landscape is also called '**Land Art**', 'Earth Art,' or '**Earthworks**'.

# Snowballs in Summer

*Snowballs in Summer* is one of Goldworthy's most famous ephemeral works. For these sculptures, he modelled thirteen giant snowballs from 'pre-millennium Scottish snow' – snow which had fallen close to his home in Scotland in the winters of 1998 and 1999. Each snowball weighed one tonne and contained different materials hidden inside. These were revealed as the snow slowly melted.

Goldsworthy placed his giant *Snowballs in Summer* in the City of London on Midsummer's Day, June 21st 2000. Some were placed near underground stations at the Barbican and Moorgate, so commuters on their way to work would see them. Others were placed where they would be discovered by chance.

The snowballs were expected to melt over three to five days in the heat of the sun. As they melted, they revealed materials including sheep's wool, crow's feathers, chestnuts, Scots pine cones, barley, barbed wire, pebbles and chalk. Some of these materials connected with the site. For example, a snowball placed near Smithfield meat market melted to reveal cow's hair and sheep's wool.

Goldsworthy's work provoked different reactions in passers-by, who were amazed to see snow melting on London streets in midsummer. The melting snowballs and the public reactions to them were recorded on a live **webcam** throughout the project.

*Goldsworthy transported snow from the Scottish mountains for his* Snowballs *project. He is shown here creating the project.*

# ANTONY GORMLEY

Antony Gormley is one of the most famous British sculptors working today. He was born in London in 1950. After going to university, he went travelling in the Middle East and India. On his return, he studied Sculpture at the Central School of Fine Art in London in 1974, Goldsmiths College (1975–77) and finally the Slade School of Fine Art (1977–79). His work first became known in the 1980s, and he has since exhibited all over the world. In 1994 Gormley won the **Turner Prize** and in 1997 he was awarded the OBE for Services to Sculpture.

## Ideas and forms

Much of Gormley's work centres on the idea of expressing the inner self through the outer body – using the **form** of the body to show emotions such as fear, grief or joy. In the 20th century, many sculptors moved away from the human form towards more **abstract** sculptures, but Gormley revived a tradition of **figurative sculpture** that stretches back to the great **Renaissance** masters like Donatello (1386–1466) and Michelangelo (1475–1564) and to the sculptors of classical Greece and Rome.

During his travels Gormley became fascinated by Indian culture and art, especially the rich tradition of sculpture that decorates temples and other public buildings. He studied **Buddhism** and meditation, and became interested in how artists used their work to express spiritual ideas and beliefs. Gormley learned the importance of just 'being' – not always thinking and doing. He wants to create art that encourages us to contemplate, and be more 'aware' and in tune with our surroundings.

## Material and techniques

Many of Gormley's works are based on casts of his own body, moulded in lead, cast in iron, or pressed in negative form into concrete. He makes a cast by covering himself with clingfilm, then cloth and plaster, and remains still until the plaster sets. He then climbs out of the plaster cast, and uses it to make a 'negative form' by pressing it in concrete, or a 'positive form' by beating and moulding sheets of lead or iron. Gormley's lead figures are hollow, and he often leaves the welded seams which join sheets of metal so they can be seen, emphasizing the way the sculpture has been constructed.

## Casting

**Casting** means making a mould (negative shape) then using a liquid material that will harden to reproduce the volume and surface of the mould. Traditionally, moulds were made from fired clay. Modern materials include concrete, hardened sand and expanded polystyrene which is burned away to leave a negative for the metal to fill.

## Angel of the North

One of Gormley's most famous sculptures is *Angel of the North* (1998), which has become a well-known landmark standing on a hilltop above an old coal mine in Tyneside. Its wide-open wings greet visitors as they reach Gateshead by the A1 road or the east coast mainline railway.

The *Angel* was **commissioned** by the City of Gateshead. Although the angel is a traditional image of western art, depicted in many paintings and sculptures made by medieval and Renaissance artists, Gormley interpreted it in a stark, modern way. He made the *Angel* from huge ribs of steel, with angular wings as long as jumbo jet wings. The *Angel* is the largest sculpture in the UK, measuring 20 metres high, with a wingspan of 54 metres.

## Designing the *Angel*

To make the sculpture, Gormley worked with a team of specialist engineers, and steel manufacturers who have constructed major bridges and oil rigs. Gormley consulted them on the construction of the *Angel* and how it would be affected by local ground conditions and wind forces.

Gormley began by making drawings and casts of the *Angel*. These were scanned onto a computer to create an electronic 3-D virtual reality *Angel*. Computerized profiling machines were then used to cut the main ribs of the body following the exact lines of Gormley's casts.

## Tools and construction

The *Angel* is constructed in three main parts – the body and two wings. Each part contains up to five different pieces:
- an external skeleton of ribs made from 50 millimetre thick steel
- a skin of 6 millimetre sheet steel that is bent and welded into the ribs that make up the body form
- ribs that lie underneath the skin plates and help shape them
- five horizontal plates of 50 millimetre steel that go right through the body
- an inner core made from a series of hollow steel cylinders and cones.

The body weighs 100 tonnes and needed a 500 tonne crane to lower it into position. The foundations were made from 150 tonnes of concrete, which anchor the sculpture into solid rock 20 metres below. The *Angel* stands on a footplate fixed by huge bolts and is built to withstand winds of over 160 km/h (99mph).

*Cranes were used to lift the enormously heavy wings into place during construction.*

When the body was in place, the wings were craned into position so that drilled steel plates lined up with plates on the body. These were welded together and fixed with 88 bolts on each side. The body and wings are constructed from special weather-resistant steel that contains some copper. This will react with the air to give the surface a mellow brown colour over the years.

> *I don't want the work to be symbolic at all, I want the work to be as actual as it can be, which is why my version of an angel is a rather uncomfortable mixture between aeronautics and anatomy.*
> ANTONY GORMLEY

## Other works

Gormley's figures are often posed to look vulnerable and alone. They are typically sited in lonely remote places such as hilltops, deserts, or tidal mud flats. For *Another Place* at Sola Beach, Stravanger, Norway (1997) he created 100 life-size iron casts of his own body, and placed them facing out to sea.

*Gormley explores man's spirituality in relation to the outside world in* Another Place *at Sola Beach, Stravanger, Norway.*

# DAMIEN HIRST

Damien Hirst is a sculptor whose work often provokes strong reactions. He was born in Bristol in 1965 and grew up in Leeds. He completed a Foundation Course at Leeds School of Art and in 1986 moved to London where he took a BA in Fine Art at Goldsmiths College. In 1988, while he was still a student, he planned and organized the Freeze exhibition of contemporary art at a London Docklands warehouse. His work became widely known when he won the **Turner Prize** in 1995. He has exhibited in Europe, the United States, Australia and Korea, holding solo exhibitions at the Institute of Contemporary Arts in London in 1991, and the Museum of Contemporary Art in Sydney in 1997, and at Charles Saatchi's gallery in County Hall, London, in 2003.

## Ideas and themes

Hirst's works include glass-tank pieces, 'cabinet sculptures', paintings and photographs. He explores disturbing themes like dying and the short span of lives. His **installations** are often controversial, as he uses shocking images and deliberately pushes the boundaries of what we see as sculpture. He regards the concept or idea of his works as all-important, and hires skilled technicians to assemble and create them. He uses engineering materials such as steel and glass, but chooses content that is charged with emotion and will provoke strong responses in his viewers.

## Influences

Many of Hirst's works show a fascination with anatomy, perhaps stemming from an interest in artists like George Stubbs (1724–1806) who specialized in detailed images of animals, particularly horses. Hirst's glass cases containing bodies or parts of dead animals are reminiscent of the work of **taxidermists** or **naturalists**. By exhibiting these works in art galleries and museums, he is breaking down the boundaries between fine art and educational displays in natural history museums, research laboratories or anatomical institutions.

## Hirst's works

For the **Venice Biennale** in 1993, Hirst made a work called *Mother and Child Divided*. The theme of mother and child is rooted in medieval and **Renaissance** images of the Virgin Mary and Jesus. He reinterpreted it using the bodies of a dead cow and calf. The animals were dissected to reveal their insides, and suspended in **formaldehyde** – a chemical solution which acts as a preservative – in glass cases. Their dead bodies, held apart forever, suggested ideas of death and separation and provoked strong reactions of shock and disgust in the viewing public.

In one work, Hirst dissected a pig's carcass and exhibited the halves in two separate tanks that the viewer could walk between. In another, a single lamb was used for an exhibit called *Away From The Flock* (1994).

In another work, *A Thousand Years* (1990), horseflies hatched out from a dead cow's head and flew briefly around before being killed by an electric fly killer. In his recent works, Hirst has taken on environmental themes. As part of a project to raise public awareness of **global warming**, he created an installation of metal cages containing empty carbon dioxide canisters that represent his own contribution to **greenhouse gas emissions**. The work is designed to be seen on the main approach to London's Gatwick Airport.

> *I want to set up situations that make people try to find meaning.*
> DAMIEN HIRST

## Cabinet pieces

Hirst often returns to the idea of a box or case containing objects chosen for their impact. His 'cabinet pieces' are small works that consist of a range of objects assembled into a case. They include the *Pharmacy* (1992) pieces, using the packaging of medicines – boxes and bottles. Hirst says he chose these items because he wanted to make art that people would believe in, as they believe in medicine.

Waste *(1994), is a form of **assemblage** sculpture, using a box or open cabinet to enclose a small world of found objects that are chosen for their texture, colour or associations. Assemblage has been practised by **Surrealist, Pop Art** and **Constructivist** sculptors.*

## The Physical Impossibility of Death in the Mind of Someone Living

Hirst's famous installation *The Physical Impossibility of Death in the Mind of Someone Living* (1991, nicknamed the 'Shark') appeared at the Royal Academy's controversial Sensation exhibition in 1997. It is one of a series of works created by Hirst that use the carcasses of animals. He preserves the bodies in a solution of the chemical formaldehyde and uses tubes connected to carbon filters to help disperse the smell of decay. Glass tanks are used to expose us to images that we could not normally see.

*I really love glass, a substance which is very solid, is dangerous but transparent. That idea of being able to see everything but not able to touch.* DAMIEN HIRST

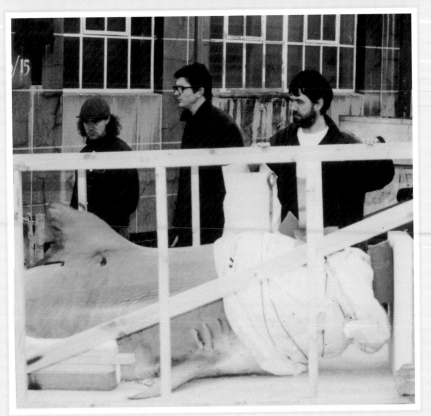

*The tiger shark had to be fully grown; its size is part of the impact that the project makes. Hirst is shown on the left, examining the newly-arrived shark.*

*I wanted the real thing, I wanted people to think 'that could eat me'.* DAMIEN HIRST

The work was **commissioned** by the collector Charles Saatchi in 1991. Hirst then paid an Australian shark hunter to catch and kill a Tiger Shark, then suspended its dead body in a tank of formaldehyde.

In this work and others like it, Hirst has said he wanted to use a thing to describe a feeling. Here, a huge shark describes the human feelings of fear and awe. It measures over 3 metres long and is bigger than the viewer. Hirst has said sharks look dead when they are alive, and alive when they are dead. This shark, although dead, looks very much alive. In the tank of green liquid, it seems to be swimming in its natural element, water. Its mouth is open, showing its huge sharp teeth. It looks as if it could kill and eat you – but the shark is dead and powerless to attack. It creates an illusion. Hirst is using the shark to remind us that we are all living under an illusion, that we will live forever; not accepting that one day every one of us will die.

# ANISH KAPOOR

Anish Kapoor creates sculptures and **installations** that inspire a sense of mystery and awe. He was born in Bombay in 1954 and grew up in India before moving to Britain in the 1970s. He studied Art at Hornsey College and then Chelsea School of Art in London. Kapoor held his first exhibition in Paris in 1980 and he has since held solo exhibitions in London and New York. His works are held in many public and private collections including the Tate Modern Gallery, London, the Museum of Modern Art, New York, the Reina Sofia, Madrid and the Stedelijk Museum, Amsterdam. He represented Britain at the **Venice Biennale** in 1990 and won the **Turner Prize** a year later.

## Ideas and forms

Kapoor is a practising **Buddhist**, and sees his works as attempting to capture feelings and experiences that are beyond words. He creates **forms** that explore opposites: light and dark, space and **void**, weight and weightlessness. To do this, he plays with scale and space, often creating works of a gigantic size using high-tech engineering techniques. He carves hollows and voids in huge blocks of stone that weigh up to 8 tonnes, and creates giant globes and funnels of polished stainless steel. Kapoor uses visual tricks that puzzle or confuse the viewer: concave mirrors that appear to suck the viewer into their space, and painted surfaces that make hard materials look like soft fabrics, or hollowed forms look solid.

In his work *When I Am Pregnant*, he made a white wall bulge into the gallery space, as if something was about to burst out of it. *Turning the World Inside Out* (1995) and *Turning the World Upside Down* were giant stainless steel globes that appeared to pull viewers inside their space; *Suck* was an enormous stainless steel funnel that seemed to disappear into the gallery floor like a giant whirlpool. These visual tricks are designed to make viewers stop and wonder.

## Influences

Kapoor's simple forms with cut-away voids and curving spaces are reminiscent of earlier British sculptors like Henry Moore and Barbara Hepworth (1903–1975). However, his work has a playful side, in the way it confuses or tricks viewers' expectations of weight, solidity or space. Colour is also an important part of Kapoor's works. His Indian heritage inspires his use of strong coloured dyes and pigments, especially powdered reds and blues.

> *The wonderful thing about colour is that it is completely non-verbal.*
> ANISH KAPOOR

# Taratantara

*Taratantara* (1999) was a temporary installation **commissioned** for the Baltic
Flour Mills building in Gateshead, UK before it was renovated as a
contemporary art gallery. Kapoor created a giant sculpture made from red PVC
(a shiny synthetic material) membrane inside the shell of the building. Kapoor
made the structure using 46 strips of PVC membrane, welded together using
radio waves. It was formed into a giant tube, suspended across the entire length
of the mill and supported at either end so that the membrane could sway in the
breeze. As viewers walked underneath, they could see glimpses of the sky
through the red throat of the membrane. Kapoor had created a new living
space inside the shell of the old building. He later used the same materials for
his vast *Marsyas* (2000) at the Tate Modern in London.

# DAVID MACH

David Mach uses cheap, mass-produced objects to construct sculptures that often combine humour with social comment. He was born in Fife in Scotland in 1956. He studied at the Duncan of Jordanstone College of Art in Dundee and the Royal College of Art, London. He has exhibited sculptures and **installations** in ten major cities including San Francisco and Melbourne.

## Materials

When Mach was a student he began making sculpture from junk and scrap materials. In the early 1980s, he developed a series of magazine installations, piling up tonnes of old printed materials such as books, telephone directories and newspapers into twisting sculptural shapes. They were installed in many different settings including a tube train, a swimming pool, a shopping centre and discotheque as well as in galleries and museums.

Mach's first public work, *Rolls Royce*, was made in Hay on Wye in 1981, using 15,000 old books. Other installations built out of magazines include ones shaped like a train, a submarine and a fireplace with smoking fire.

> They [magazine installations] are made with tonnes and tonnes of magazines and newspapers, both of which come to us every day in their zillions, in a bombardment of information. They are like the physical **manifestation** of airwaves ... a kind of junk mail hell or Internet highway pile up. DAVID MACH

For his work the *Temple at Tyre* in Edinburgh, Mach used 6000 old car tyres. Rubber tyres were also used to make *Polaris*, a sculpture of a nuclear submarine that was shown at the Hayward Gallery in London in 1983.

Although they are constructed from cheap, throwaway materials, some of Mach's works are on an awe-inspiring scale, such as the giant classical pillars that he constructed from newspapers and magazines for the Tramway Gallery, Glasgow in 1990.

## Match heads

Mach has worked on a smaller scale to make his *Match heads*. This is a series of heads in the style of Chinese and Venetian theatre masks, made from unstruck matches glued together so that coloured heads show on the surface. Mach made the first *Match head* in 1982, after a reviewer compared one of his magazine installations to matchstick models of the Eiffel Tower. The head accidentally caught fire, so that the colours burned away into shades of grey. Mach deliberately used this for later *Match heads*, making them into **Performance Art** as the matches burned, changing the colours in the head.

*This picture of one of Mach's match head projects,* Zebra Matchhead No 5 *(1997) shows how his sculptures transform into a different type of art and change appearance when lit.*

## Influences

In the 20th century, artists began using everyday materials to create sculptures. The German **Dadaist** artist Kurt Schwitters (1887–1948) was one of the first artists to use cheap, scrap materials from everyday life in his collage works. He collected rubbish such as used bus tickets, stamps, hair and old catalogues which he assembled into collages. Later, he used pieces of junk to make **Constructivist** sculptures. Picasso (see page 4) created **figurative** work using 'found objects' such as bits of scrap metal or pieces of junk like old saucepans, toy cars and bicycle handlebars.

# Spaceman

*Spaceman* (2000), is one of Mach's coat hanger pieces. These works include vases, portraits, busts and figures made from hundreds of metal coat hangers. The hangers are cheap and disposable, but the method Mach uses to shape them into a sculpture requires lots of time and detailed effort. Each coat hanger has to be individually shaped and bent and welded several times to its neighbour. *Spaceman* took six months to create. It was exhibited in the Walking Man Exhibition in the gardens of the Palais Royal in Paris.

> *Coat hangers come from the same line as matches. They are like nothing, you pay them no attention, they have no value, if anything they are an irritant brought back from the dry cleaners.*
> DAVID MACH

*Spaceman* was inspired by Mach's childhood memories of the television pictures of Neil Armstrong walking on the Moon in 1969. Mach was interested by the idea of representing this global image of advanced science and technology using a cheap, familiar everyday object – the coat hanger.

The black and white television images of the first moon landing were blurred, and the time-lapse effect of the live broadcast meant that as Armstrong moved, he left a ghostly image behind. Mach recreates this effect by using the hooks of hundreds of coat hangers to create an aura or haze around the spaceman figure. If the viewer touches any of the hooks, the sculpture will vibrate, creating a blurred image. The coat hanger hooks form a kind of protective armour as well as suggesting the ghostly television image. They also remind us of radio or television aerials, as if the figure is alert and 'wired up' to radio waves and signals.

Spaceman *is so large that the artist had to use a platform to work on it. Here we can see the fibreglass mould being sculpted.*

*The hooks make a ghost out of the object from which they protrude. This mass of hooks coupled with a movement because the sculptures have an incredible spring in them provides a kind of aura around the object. Movement and the hooks make a kind of visual vibration. It's like watching a string being plucked on a piano.*
DAVID MACH

## Technique

Mach's first coat hanger sculpture was a mask of Hugh Cornwell, the lead singer and songwriter for the band, The Stranglers. He began by **modelling** the head, then made a mould of it to create a hard plastic form. The coat hangers were shaped and welded around this form – Mach's usual method.

Mach modelled the figure of the *Spaceman* in clay. He used a fibreglass mould to create the hard plastic form onto which he could bend and weld the coat hangers. When the form is taken away, the coat hangers have a springy quality that gives the sculpture movement and life.

# CORNELIA PARKER

Cornelia Parker is a British sculptor whose works include **installations**, slide projections and sculptures. She was born in Cheshire in 1956. Her works have been shown at the Serpentine Gallery and Tate Modern in London, and in Vienna, Paris and Berlin. She also has works in many private and public collections and was short listed for the **Turner Prize** in 1997.

## Transforming materials

Since the 1980s, Parker has become known for installations made from materials put through violent acts of transformation. She takes ordinary, everyday objects, such as coins or cutlery and has them flattened, crushed, or exploded so that we see them in a new way. She has flattened coins under the wheels of a passing train, steam-rolled over silver tableware, blown up a garden shed and its contents, and thrown objects off the White Cliffs of Dover.

Parker then constructs her sculptures and installations from the resulting debris. Many of the works are suspended in a gallery space using black wires or string so that we see the shattered pieces from which they are made in a new light; from a new angle. Once-solid objects that have been crushed or blown apart become delicate, fragmented works. Often the works have a quiet, dream-like quality, in spite of their violent creation.

*My work is somehow very quiet and not really violent at all – it's calm, like the eye of the storm.* CORNELIA PARKER

Parker enjoys the idea of making works that she can re-hang in different locations, giving them the opportunity to look different in different lights and settings. She chooses materials that carry their own associations and ideas, but which are re-invented by the way she transforms them. *Thirty Pieces of Silver* (1988–89) was made from around a thousand pieces of silver plate, crushed by a steamroller then suspended in 30 pools like water lilies. *Hanging Fire* (1998) was made from pieces of charcoal from the ruins of an old factory. *Edge of England* (1999) was made from chalk that had fallen from the cliffs at Beachy Head off the south coast of England.

## Cold Dark Matter: An Exploded View

Parker made the work *Cold Dark Matter: An Exploded View* in 1991. It has been described as a sculptural 'Big Bang.' It was once an ordinary garden shed and its contents. Parker filled the shed with junk collected from garden sheds and bought at car boot sales. She chose familiar objects that we associate with the traditional, mid 20th-century British way of life – a school satchel, a garden fork, a pair of Wellington boots. The shed was photographed in a white-painted gallery in London's east end. Parker then had the shed and its contents taken away and blown up by the British Army. Having the shed and its very British contents literally blown apart by the army – the official defender of the British way of life – is typical of Parker's delight in opposites; she sets up contrasting or opposing ideas in the same work.

## Displaying the wreckage

Parker collected the wreckage from the explosion and reassembled it in a white room in the Tate Gallery, London. The shattered debris was suspended in space from wires, as if frozen at the moment of explosion. At the centre were tiny fragments of a toy car, plastic hair curlers and a tin can. Around the edges were larger pieces such as shattered planks of wood and a bicycle wheel. A single light bulb hung in the middle so that shadows of the exploded debris were cast around the gallery walls – adding to the sense of movement.

The title refers to the 'cold dark matter' that scientists are unable to measure in the universe. Something that is mysterious and cannot be measured is here presented in an 'exploded view' – a term which is used to describe technical diagrams in manuals for cars and household machines. These diagrams show how different parts fit together: they are labelled and measured, in a way that 'cold dark matter' never can be.

> *Cold dark matter is the material within the universe that we cannot see and we cannot quantify. We know it exists but we can't measure it. It's immeasurable, unfathomable.* CORNELIA PARKER

## Other works

In 1997, Parker created *Mass (Colder Darker Matter)* which was exhibited at the Tate Gallery in London and short listed for the Turner Prize. The work was constructed from the blackened remains of a church in Texas, in the United States, that had been struck by lightning and burned down. Fragments of charcoal were suspended in a weightless, **abstract** mass using wire and black string.

One of Parker's most well-known works, *Breathless* (2001), was commissioned by the Victoria and Albert Museum (V&A) in London. For this work, Parker purchased 54 old brass instruments from the **Salvation Army** and the **British Legion**. She then had them crushed by one of the vast weight-bearing machines that raises and lowers Tower Bridge in London. The flattened instruments were suspended from wires in a circular space that was once a floor between galleries in the V&A, so that the installation could be viewed from above or below. As with the earlier works, its theme is opposites – brass instruments, once so noisy, are now silent.

I wanted to explore the ideas of duality; light/dark, silence/noise,
upper class/lower class, the North/South divide, black cloud/silver
lining, death/resurrection.
CORNELIA PARKER, *describing her motive for making* Breathless.

## Influences

The American Alexander Calder (1898–1976) was one of the first sculptors to
experiment with 'suspended' works – by using metal wire to mark out
pinpoints in space and create moving sculptures. In 1931, he designed a
sculpture made from steel wires and counter weights that moved constantly in
the air currents. Marcel Duchamp (see page 5) called it a **mobile**.

# ROBERT SMITHSON

Robert Smithson is famous for his huge outdoor 'Earthworks', a form of sculpture in the landscape. Smithson was born in Passaic, New Jersey, USA in 1938. He studied at the Art Students' League and held his first one-man exhibition as a painter in New York in 1959. As well as Earthworks, Smithson's work includes film, video, writing and photography.

## Ideas and materials

Smithson began working in the **Minimalist** style in the 1960s, creating block-like steel structures and 'wall works' using metal frames containing mirrorized plastic, which played with light and reflections. In the late 1960s, he began to concentrate on **Conceptual Art**, in which the artist's idea is all-important. He began a series of works called *Sites* and *Non-Sites*, which combined his interests in landscape, natural history, geology and maps. The *Non-Sites* used natural waste in the same way that junk artists had used urban waste. Smithson assembled debris and rocks from remote sites with plans of the site, geological maps, instamatic photographs and mirrors.

Smithson visited old urban and industrial sites including quarries and mine workings in Pennsylvania and New Jersey, and collected fragments of rock, gravel and geological refuse which he arranged in random heaps or in metal or wooden bins. For *A Non-site, Pine Barrens, New Jersey* (1968), he chose materials from the ruins of old buildings, and arranged them in bins with maps of the site. As these works were exhibited in galleries or museums, they brought elements of the landscape indoors.

Smithson was especially interested in sites that showed evidence of work, time and decay.

> *I began in a very primitive way … certain sites would appeal to me more – sites that had been in some way disrupted … pulverised.*
> ROBERT SMITHSON

## Working in the landscape

By the early 1970s, Smithson had moved his work entirely outside the gallery. He wanted his work to be in the landscape where it would be exposed and changed by the forces of water, wind and weather. He began to create huge Earthworks in remote settings, which meant they would be known and seen mainly from aerial film or photography.

# Spiral Jetty

The most famous of Smithson's Earthworks is *Spiral Jetty*, which he created at Rozel Point, Great Salt Lake, Utah in 1970. This site appealed to Smithson because it is remote and desolate. The landscape is littered with industrial wreckage and vehicles abandoned after attempts to extract oil from tar deposits. After selecting the site, Smithson made numerous drawings and plans, based around a spiral form. This design made the form of the jetty echo the natural form of the salt crystals that coat the rocks here.

Smithson's monumental earthwork is a spiral road measuring 460 metres long and 4.5 metres wide. It is constructed from the local black basalt rock and earth, and stretches anti-clockwise into the red water of the lake.

## Tools and techniques

Smithson's work on *Spiral Jetty* was funded by the gallery owner and art patron Virginia Dwan. To construct it, he needed 6650 tons of black basalt, limestone rocks and local earth. The rock and earth was moved into place by building contractors using trucks and industrial earthmoving machines.

Smithson had deliberately chosen a remote site, but to make the image of *Spiral Jetty* accessible to everyone, he filmed the trucks and diggers at work. He also recorded *Spiral Jetty's* construction in drawings and photographs, and in an essay he wrote two years after it was completed.

When he was working on *Spiral Jetty*, the water level of the lake was unusually low. Two years after its completion, water levels rose, flooding the sculpture. But it has since reappeared during periods of drought, as in 2002.

> *In its scale and ideas, this sculpture embodies the spirit of some of the great monuments of past civilizations, yet it is utterly contemporary in concept and execution.*
> NANCY HOLT – Smithson's wife

## Influences

*Spiral Jetty* was inspired by the Great Serpent Mound, a Pre-Columbian Indian monument in south-west Ohio which looks like a snake swallowing an egg. Early Amerindian earthworks are typically conical or linear mounds. They were probably religious effigies (images) and were used as burial sites for important people like chiefs and priests. The first mound builders were the Adena Indians, hunter-gatherers who settled on the American continent 2000 years ago.

The Great Serpent near Chillicothe, Ohio, is one of the most spectacular mound effigies. It lies on a ridge overlooking the valley of Bush Creek and is believed to date from around 1100 BC. The body of the serpent is a long, rounded mound averaging a metre in height and almost 6 metres wide. It stretches to nearly a quarter of a mile long. The mound is constructed of rock and clay, outlined with small stones and clay. The serpent was probably a religious symbol, and may have been constructed to ward off evil or as a tribute to a god.

*The Great Serpent Mound in south-west Ohio is shown here. The snake shape can be seen clearly.*

## The concept of Earthworks

The new form of sculpture in the landscape, called Earthworks, or **Land Art**, was developed in the late 1960s and early 1970s by Smithson, Robert Morris and others. The artist used elements of nature found on the site, or rearranged the landscape using earthmoving equipment. The resulting work was deliberately exposed to the weather and natural forces such as wind and water erosion.

> *Instead of putting a work of art on some land, some land is put into the work of art.* ROBERT SMITHSON

## Amarillo Ramp

Smithson went on to explore the themes of time and decay in *Amarillo Ramp*, which he began to construct on the shores of an irrigation lake. But in 1973, he was killed when his plane crashed in Texas while he was surveying the site. The work was completed after his death by his wife and friends.

# RACHEL WHITEREAD

Rachel Whiteread is a sculptor who creates casts from the spaces inside and around objects. She was born in 1963 in London, UK. She studied Painting at Brighton Polytechnic then trained as a sculptor under Antony Gormley (see pages 20–29) at the Slade School of Fine Art in London, from 1985 to 1987. She held her first solo exhibition in 1988 at the Carlyle gallery in London, and her works have since been exhibited in Europe and the USA. She won the **Turner Prize** in 1993, and a medal at the **Venice Biennale** in 1997.

## Materials

The traditional materials for **casting** (see page 20) are bronze and lead, but modern sculptors have experimented with different materials including concrete, aluminium and different types of plastics such as resins. Resins can be coloured, and opaque or translucent. They are built-up in coats or layers in the mould, and an agent is added to release them from the mould. Whiteread works in a range of materials including plaster, concrete, rubber, resin and polystyrene.

## Re-inventing an old technique

Whiteread has re-invented the technique of casting, making casts not of objects, but of the spaces inside and around them: *Untitled (Torso)* (1991) was cast from the inside of a hot water bottle. Her casts of ordinary household objects such as bathtubs, mattresses, tables and chairs are like ghostly echoes of the originals. Critics have described her works as 'solidifying space'. She records every detail of the space in her casts, making them ghostly imprints that evoke memory, loss and the passing of time.

## Early sculptures

For her early sculptures, made in the late 1980s, Whiteread chose objects that carried sentimental associations. *Yellow Leaf* (1989) was cast from a table that reminded her of the table in her grandmother's kitchen. To echo the domestic theme, she used cooking oil – an everyday ingredient from a kitchen store cupboard – as a 'release agent'. This separated the cast from the table. The oil transferred the imprint of every detail from the table to the cast, such as traces of yellow colouring, and even dirt like dust and chewing gum. In this way, Whiteread's casts carry imprints of the people and lives that have used or occupied them.

*Ghost* was a complete cast of an entire room from a Victorian house, which Whiteread cast in plaster for the Freeze show in London's Docklands in 1988, organized by Damien Hirst (see page 24). The house was similar to the one in which she had grown up. Whiteread said she wanted to 'mummify the air in a room.'

Whiteread cast the work by hand, working on each side of the room in turn, then taking the panels back to her studio and fixing them to a framework. The cast was a negative impression of the room: the space inside the room had been made into solid form. Every detail, such as window frames, light sockets, gas fires, even traces of old wallpaper and paint, was imprinted on the cast.

## House

Whiteread's most famous work is *House*, which won the Turner Prize in 1993. It was a complete cast of the inside of a three-storey, Victorian, terraced house at 193, Grove Road, Bow, East London. The house was the last in a row that was being knocked down for re-development. Whiteread's idea was to record the space where generations of people had lived. She wanted to make a cast that would record the feeling of the house, the memories that people had of living there, and the traces of their lives.

## Working method

The work was funded by James Lingwood of Artangel, an art-**commissioning** organization. Before making the cast, Whiteread took photographs of the house and talked to the last family who had lived there. For the casting, she worked with a team of experts who used a technique called gunniting. This means creating a solid skin by spraying concrete. Each room was cast separately, and new foundations built to support the concrete cast. Once it had cured (set hard) the house walls were demolished to reveal the cast. As with *Ghost*, every detail including light switches and ceiling roses, was recorded. The sculpture stood in Grove Road for three months before it was destroyed.

*Whiteread working on site on* House.

## Influences

Whiteread's works have a simplicity of **form** which is influenced by American **Minimalist** and **Conceptual** Art of the 1960s and 70s, especially the works of Bruce Nauman (b. 1941), Eva Hesse (1936–70), Carl André and Richard Serra. In the 1980s, she became interested in the idea of making casts of 'negative spaces', such as the space underneath a piece of furniture. The first sculptor to do this was Bruce Nauman in the 1960s with *A cast of the space under my chair* (1965–68).

## Other works

For *Untitled (One Hundred Spaces)* which was exhibited at the Sensation exhibition at the Royal Academy in 1997, Whiteread made a hundred casts of the space underneath a chair, using different coloured resins, echoing Bruce Nauman's work from the 1960s.

Whiteread also made casts of library shelves for the Holocaust Memorial which **commemorates** the thousands of Austrian Jews killed in the World War II. *Nameless Library* (2000) stands in the Judenplatz in Vienna. It is a concrete rectangle, lined from floor to ceiling with shelves of books with their pages turned outwards. At one end are massive double doors cast in concrete, giving it the appearance of a tomb. The books may be seen as representing all the lost lives: potential scientists, artists, writers, whose lives will never be 'read'.

Another public work was the *Monument for Trafalgar Square* (2001). This was a giant clear resin cast standing on the empty plinth in the Square. It was the largest casting in plastic ever made (it was 4.3 metres high). The monument attracted lots of attention from the media and was seen by millions of people. It stood in Trafalgar Square from June 2001 until May 2002.

> *After spending time in Trafalgar Square observing the people, traffic, pigeons, architecture, sky and fountains, I became acutely aware of the general chaos of central London life. I decided that the most appropriate sculpture for the place would be to make a 'pause' a quiet moment for space.* RACHEL WHITEREAD

# MADELINE WIENER

Madeline Wiener has been carving stone for over 30 years, working from her studio in Denver, Colorado, USA. She was born in 1947 and studied at the New York School of Visual Arts (1968–74). In recent years, she has concentrated on making large-scale public works, for **commissions** in different locations in the USA and overseas, including India and Scotland.

## Materials and techniques

Wiener works in different kinds of stone, including Colorado marble, granite, dolomite and sandstone. To **carve** them, she uses a combination of traditional hand tools and modern power tools. When she is working, Wiener needs to wear protective gear such as safety glasses, hearing protectors and a respirator to stop her breathing in rock dust.

Wiener uses high-tech power tools such as a diamond chain saw and 23 centimetre diamond blades to block out the main shapes. This is called 'roughing out.' More stone is removed as she cuts into the stone, creating a series of grooves with small slices of stone in between. She then works with a combination of pneumatic drills and other power tools, as well as a traditional hammer and chisel to shape the stone. It is then filed, sanded and polished to achieve the final surface.

## Combining traditional and modern techniques

In 1999, Wiener was invited to a granite **symposium** in Adichunchangira, a remote village in southern India. Here she worked with a group of stone carvers who were making sculptures for the local medical school. Wiener worked with modern power tools, alongside local Tamil sculptors who used hammers and chisels in the traditional way to carve the architectural details of a new temple. This commission reflects her interest in using sculpture to encourage cultural exchange and bringing together traditional and modern techniques of working with stone.

### Stone carving

Carving hard stone calls for control and planning. Sculptors first plan their work using drawings and clay models. When they have chosen a block of stone, it may need to be split then marked up for carving using a pointing machine, which measures the depth at which the stone must be cut away at different points. The two traditional methods of carving are cutting with a chisel, and abrading, which means pounding the stone then rubbing it with an abrasive stone such as emery.

# Family Reflections

*Family Reflections* (2000) is part of a series of sculptures called *Bench People*. These stone sculptures have seats built into simplified **figurative** forms. Each represents a seated or reclining figure reading.

*Family Reflections* is carved from a 12,250 kilogram block of Colorado marble. Wiener wanted to create a sculpture that was not just visually pleasing, but one that would invite people to touch its cool surface, rest on it and enjoy the feeling of the marble as they sit or climb on it. Each figure represents a mother, father and child.

## Themes and intentions

For *Family Reflections*, Wiener's theme is the family and in particular the way family members support each other. The mother and father are leaning into one another and looking against each other. The child is looking up at the father, and leaning against him to show how each member of the family depends on each other.

The sculpture was installed in December 2000 outside the Scripps Memorial Hospital for Family Health Care in La Jolla, California. Sited between a fountain and the main entrance to the hospital, it is intended as a place staff, patients and their families can go for rest and comfort.

*Wiener worked on the sculpture with the help of her family and friends – here she is shown working on* Family Reflections *with her son.*

> *I feel that [by] enticing the viewer to become part of the work itself and interacting with it … continues the tactile, creative process, thus making each work complete.* MADELINE WIENER

## Colorado marble

Colorado Yule Marble comes from the quarries in Marble, Colorado, high in the Rocky Mountains near the ski resort of Aspen. It is the marble used for famous memorials such as the *Lincoln Memorial* in Washington D.C. and the *Tomb of the Unknown Soldier* in London. Working with marble is physically challenging. It is a dense material, weighing up to 3 tonnes per cubic metre.

To block out the **forms** of *Family Reflections*, Wiener worked with a diamond chain saw and other power tools. The sculpture was begun in the studio, then transported on a truck to be completed close to its final site.

## Public works

In her work for public places, Wiener's aim is to create interactive sculptures that invite people to sit or climb on the sculpture, and to touch the stone and respond to the way it feels. In Scotland, she used sandstone for her sculpture *Symbiosis*, which is set on the corner of a busy roundabout in Livingston. Another sculpture, *Sharing*, is set below the Town Hall in Hamilton, and shows two women doing laundry, as they would have done in the public washing baths in the past.

## Influences

Wiener's work is influenced by the simple, primitive shapes of Stone Age sculpture such as the marble figures carved by the early Greek culture (2700–2300 BC). Wiener is also inspired by 20th century sculptors such as Henry Moore and Constantin Brancusi (1876–1957). They wanted to create simple, **organic** forms that would bring out the beauty of their materials. For inspiration, Henry Moore looked to primitive sculptures and also to natural forms such as pebbles, stones and shells. In the 1930s, he began to create semi-**abstract**, rounded forms that displayed the natural properties of his materials – stone, bronze or wood. He represented the theme of the family in many large seated and reclining figures.

# TIMELINE

| | |
|---|---|
| *c.*21,000BC | Sculpture has its beginnings in carved stone, bone and ivory figures and in cave art |
| *c.*2700BC | Early Greek (Cycladic) marble sculpture starts to be created |
| *c.*500BC | Classical Greek sculpture in marble and bronze is being created |
| *c.*240–210BC | Chinese Terracotta Army, the 6000 life-size clay warriors who 'protected' the tomb of the first emperor of China, is built |
| 150BC | *Venus de Milo*, a famous Classical statue, is made |
| 900–500 | Easter Island Heads carved by the peoples of Rapa Nui |
| *c.*1408–9 | Donatello's bronze *David* |
| 1501 | Michelangelo's marble *David* |
| 1881 | Pablo Picasso is born |
| 1886 | Rodin's *The Kiss* |
| 1887 | Marcel Duchamp is born |
| 1890 | Russian **Constructivist**, Naum Gabo is born |
| 1895 | First **Venice Biennale** – exhibition of contemporary art – is held |
| 1898 | Henry Moore is born |
| 1904 | **Surrealist** painter Salvador Dali is born |
| 1908 | Henry Moore is born |
| 1911 | Louise Bourgeois is born |
| 1913 | Duchamp's *Bicycle Wheel* is created |
| | Boccioni's *Unique Forms of Continuity in Space* |
| 1914–18 | World War I speeds up processes of change in society and industry |
| 1917 | Marcel Duchamp's *Fountain* |
| 1920 | Constructivist Manifesto is published in Russia |
| 1931 | Alexander Calder's *Mobile* |
| 1938 | Robert Smithson is born |
| 1939–45 | World War II. Some European artists emigrate to the USA, and New York emerges after the war as a leading art centre |

| 1950 | Antony Gormley is born |
|---|---|
| 1952 | George VI dies; Princess Elizabeth becomes Queen Elizabeth II |
| 1954 | Anish Kapoor is born |
| 1956 | David Mach is born; Cornelia Parker is born; Madeline Wiener is born |
| 1958 | Sokari Douglas Camp is born |
| 1960s | **Land Art** or **Earthworks** take sculpture outside |
| 1963 | Rachel Whiteread is born |
| 1965 | Damien Hirst is born |
| 1973 | Pablo Picasso dies |
| | Robert Smithson dies |
| 1972 | Carl André's *Equivalent VIII* (nicknamed Tate Bricks) is created. It consists of 120 stacked bricks and becomes a symbol for the baffling nature of modern art in the 1970s. |
| 1984 | First **Turner Prize** is awarded |
| 1985 | Saatchi Gallery opens in London |
| 1988 | *Freeze* exhibition opens in London |
| 1990 | Anish Kapoor represents Britain at the Venice Biennale |
| 1991 | Anish Kapoor wins the Turner Prize |
| 1993 | Rachel Whiteread wins the Turner Prize |
| 1994 | Antony Gormley wins the Turner Prize |
| 1995 | Damien Hirst wins the Turner Prize |
| 1997 | Sensation exhibition at the Royal Academy, London |
| | Antony Gormley wins the OBE for Services to Sculpture |
| | Rachel Whiteread wins medal at the Venice Biennale |
| 2000 | Tate Modern opens in London |
| 2002 | Anish Kapoor's *Marsyas*, possibly the world's biggest indoor sculpture, shown at Tate Modern, London |

# GLOSSARY

**abstract** sculpture or painting that does not represent figures or objects

**assemblage** making sculpture from lots of different parts or materials

**British Legion** charity for men and women who have served in the British Armed Forces

**Buddhism** world religion that began in India. Buddhists follow the teachings of Siddhartha Gautama, known as the Buddha.

**carving** cutting or chipping away a material to make a shape from it

**casting** making sculpture using a mould and a material that will harden to reproduce the volume and surface of the mould

**classical sculpture** sculpture created by the ancient Greeks and Romans

**commemorative** work of art created as a tribute to a person or people who have died

**commission** work that is produced as the result of a specific request from a buyer

**Conceptual Art** art based on the concept that artists' ideas are more important than the actual appearance of the art

**construction** building a sculpture from separate parts

**Constructivism** style of art that developed in Russia based on abstract forms and modern engineering materials

**Cubism** art movement developed by Picasso and Braque in the early 1900s, with its roots in theories put forward by Paul Cézanne (1839–1906). Cubists aimed to analyse the structure or form of objects by expressing them in geometrical shapes.

**Dadaism** art movement founded in 1915 that went against traditional notions of art, often leaving everything to chance

**Earthworks** moving or shaping the natural landscape into art

**figurative sculpture** sculpture that represents figures or objects

**formaldehyde** chemical solution that preserves things, usually humans or animals

**forms** shapes, either two-dimensional or three-dimensional

**Futurism** art movement that began in 1909 which was inspired by the speed and machinery of modern life

**global warming** gradual heating up of the Earth due to pollution

**greenhouse gas emissions** leakage of types of gas that destroy the Earth's atmosphere (ozone layer)

**Happenings** form of art based on live performances

**installation art** work of art that is put together or 'installed' in a room or space (indoors or outdoors) which relies on the space as part of its effect

**interventions** ways in which an artist makes changes to nature

**kinetic art sculpture** sculpture that involves movement

**Land Art** using the natural environment to create art

**manifestation** sign or indication

**Masquerade** Performance Art celebrating a change of season or time in a person's life

**Minimalism** movement in art based on simple pure forms, often geometric and large, or colours

**mobile** suspended or moving sculpture

**modelling** making sculpture by building up a soft material like wax or clay

**naturalists** people who study nature and wildlife

**organic** made from, or based on, living forms in nature

**patron** someone who gives financial (or other) support to an artist or gallery

**Performance Art** art that is acted out live in front of an audience

**Pop Art** art movement of the 1960s based on popular images and objects. Artists associated with Pop Art include Richard Hamilton, David Hockney, Roy Lichtenstein and Andy Warhol.

**relief sculpture** sculpture carved onto a surface

**Renaissance** French word meaning 'rebirth', referring to changes in European culture between the late 14th and early 17th centuries. A 're-birth' of the arts began in Italy.

**retrospective** exhibition that looks back at an artist's life and works

**Salvation Army** Christian organization and charity

**site specific (sculpture)** sculpture designed for a particular site or place

**sublime** inspiring feelings of awe or wonder

**Surrealism** art movement starting in Europe in the 1920s that explored the world of dreams and the subconcious

**symposium** a meeting of experts who come together to discuss and study their special subject

**taxidermists** people who preserve birds and animals by stuffing them and using special chemicals

**Turner Prize** annual prize awarded to contemporary artists in Britain

**Venice Biennale** contemporary art show held every two years in Venice

**void** hole or empty space

**webcam** digital camera that is linked up to the Internet

# KEY WORKS

**LOUISE BOURGEOIS**
*Maman* (1990)
*Cells* (1990–93)
*I do, I undo, I redo* (1999)

**SOKARI DOUGLAS CAMP**
*Naked Fish* (1998)
*Big Masquerade with Boat and Household* (1995)

**ANDY GOLDSWORTHY**
*Sheepfolds* (1996–2000)
*Snowballs in Summer* (2000)

**ANTONY GORMLEY**
*Another Place* (1997)
*Field* series (1993)
*Angel of the North* (1998)

**DAMIEN HIRST**
*The Physical Impossibility of Death in the Mind of Someone Living* (1991)
*Mother and Child Divided* (1993)
*Away from the Flock* (1994)

**ANISH KAPOOR**
*Taratantara* (1999)
*Marsyas* (2000)

**DAVID MACH**
*Match Head* series (1982– )
*Spaceman* (2000)

**CORNELIA PARKER**
*Cold Dark Matter: An Exploded View* (1991)
*Breathless* (2001)
*Thirty Pieces of Silver* (1988–89)

**ROBERT SMITHSON**
*Spiral Jetty* (1970)
*Non-site* series (1968)

**RACHEL WHITEREAD**
*Ghost* (1998)
*House* (1993)
*Nameless Library* (2000)

**MADELINE WIENER**
*Family Reflections* (2000)

# WHERE TO SEE WORKS

Here are galleries and public places where the works of art mentioned in this book can be seen. Ring to find out what is showing before you go:

*Goodwood House, UK* – Sculpture at Goodwood has works by Andy Goldsworthy and Rachel Whiteread

*Hamilton and Livingston, UK* – these towns in Scotland house works by Madeline Wiener

*Henry Moore Foundation, Perry Green, Hertfordshire, UK* – houses works by Henry Moore

*Hepworth Museum and Sculpture Garden, St Ives, UK* – houses a collection of works by Barbara Hepworth

*Institute of Contemporary Arts, The Mall, London, UK* – holds exhibitions, films and talks about contemporary arts, including sculpture

*New Art Centre Sculpture Park and Gallery, Salisbury, UK* – features sculpture and contemporary art

*Nottingham Playhouse, Nottingham, UK* – holds works by Anish Kapoor

*Tate Modern, London, UK* – The Tate Modern collections include works by Anthony Gormley, Damien Hirst, David Mach, Louise Bourgeois, Cornelia Parker, Rachel Whiteread, Robert Smithson and Anish Kapoor

*The Museum of Contemporary Art, Sydney, Australia* – features sculpture and contemporary art

*The Museum of Modern Art, New York, USA* – features sculpture and contemporary art

*Unilever Collection, London, UK* – holds contemporary and African works including sculptures by Sokari Douglas Camp

Victoria and Albert Museum, London, UK – holds work by Cornelia Parker

The following web sites show sculptures by the artists featured in this book:

http://www.sokari.co.uk – Sokari Douglas Camp
http://www.davidmach.com – David Mach
http://www.gateshead.gov.uk/angel – Antony Gormley's *Angel of the North*
http://www.madelinewiener.com – Madeline Wiener
http://www.robertsmithson.com – Robert Smithson
http://www.tate.org.uk

# FURTHER READING

*Antony Gormley,* J. Hutchinson (Phaidon, 2000)
*Contemporary Outdoor Sculpture,* Barrie Brooke (Rockport, 1999)
*Encyclopaedia of Sculpture Techniques,* John Mills (Batsford, 1990)
*Sculpture since 1945,* Andrew Causey (OUP, 1998)

# INDEX